Kristi
Yamaguchi

Kristi Yamaguchi

artist on ice

Shiobhan Donohue

Lerner Publications Company ■ Minneapolis

With love to Kathleen Donohue and Abbie Burke

A glossary of figure skating terms begins on page 62.

This book is available in two bindings:
Library binding by Lerner Publications Company
Soft cover by First Avenue Editions
241 First Avenue North
Minneapolis, MN 55401

LIBRARY OF CONGRESS CATALOGING-IN-PUBLICATION DATA

Donohue, Shiobhan.
 Kristi Yamaguchi: artist on ice/Shiobhan Donohue.
  p. cm.
 Summary: A biography of the figure skater who won the
National, Olympic, and World Championships in 1992.
 ISBN 0-8225-0522-3 (library edition)
 ISBN 0-8225-9649-0 (paperback)
 1. Yamaguchi, Kristi—Juvenile literature. 2. Skaters—United
States—Biography—Juvenile literature. [1. Yamaguchi, Kristi.
2. Ice skaters. 3. Japanese Americans—biography.] I. Title.
GV850.Y36D65 1994
796.91'092—dc20
[B]   92-38272

International Standard Book Number: 0-8225-0522-3 (lib. bdg.)
International Standard Book Number: 0-8225-9649-0 (pbk.)

Manufactured in the United States of America
4 5 6 7 8 9 – P/JR – 01 00 99 98 97 96

Contents

1
Triple Crown

The rhythmic Spanish music "Malaguena" filled the arena in Oakland, California. Five-foot tall, 93-pound Kristi Yamaguchi, competing in the World Figure Skating Championships, skated across the ice. She flowed from one element to the next, completing six difficult three-revolution jumps. "I didn't think about expecting to win," Kristi said. "I thought about skating as well as I did at the Olympics."

Kristi's hometown of Fremont, California, is a short distance from Oakland. She said, "It was the most exciting experience to see so many people I knew, so many friends and family...their energy transferred to me on the ice."

Kristi attempted all the movements she planned in her four-minute show. When she finished, the spirited crowd of 10,000 stood and applauded. A group of young skaters helped "Yama," as she is known to her friends, gather flowers and stuffed animals thrown onto the ice.

The judges awarded Kristi nearly perfect scores of 5.9 (out of a possible 6.0), placing her first among the 24 skaters. On this day, March 29, 1992, Kristi became the first American woman, since Peggy Fleming in 1968, to win the World Championships two years in a row.

Kristi also became the first American woman, since Dorothy Hamill in 1976, to win the "triple crown" of figure skating—the national, Olympic, and world championship titles all in one year. "I've dreamed about this since I was a little girl and first put on a pair of skates," Kristi said. "To think of how far I've come...it's all still sinking in."

Kristi remembered watching Dorothy Hamill skate at the 1976 Winter Olympics. "It's kind of neat to think I'm following in her footsteps, because she was always a big idol of mine," Kristi said. "Part of the reason why I'm in the sport is because of her. She was an inspiration to start figure skating."

Kristi also thought of the events that had occurred since she won the gold medal at the Winter Olympics in Albertville, France: the parade in Fremont, dinner at the White House with President George Bush and Russian leader Boris Yeltsin, an appearance on "The Arsenio Hall

Show," photo sessions for magazines and posters, and requests for autographs. She knew the future would bring more exciting changes.

Olympian Dorothy Hamill

In 1992 Kristi Yamaguchi stood at the top of the figure skating world.

At the medal ceremony following the World Championships, "The Star-Spangled Banner" was played in Kristi's honor. She led the other medalists, America's Nancy Kerrigan and China's Chen Lu, on a skate around the Oakland Coliseum. Waving and laughing, Kristi smiled at her parents, Jim and Carole, her older sister, Lori, and her younger brother, Brett. Kristi treasured the moment of her victory. She was now Kristi Yamaguchi—national, Olympic, and world figure skating champion.

10

2
Warming Up

Kristi Tsuya Yamaguchi was born on July 12, 1971, in Hayward, California (near San Francisco). She is the second child of Carole and Jim Yamaguchi. Kristi's mother is a medical secretary, and her father is a dentist.

Kristi began skating at age six, one year after watching Dorothy Hamill win a gold medal at the 1976 Winter Olympics. Kristi saw her in ice shows and television specials. She wanted to learn to skate like Dorothy.

Kristi's mother encouraged her daughter's interest in ice-skating—but not because she wanted Kristi to become a champion. The Yamaguchis thought skating might help strengthen Kristi's legs.

Always a performer, Kristi liked ballet and cheerleading as a young girl.

Kristi had been born with clubfoot—a condition in which her foot turned severely inward. This ailment had to be corrected before she could walk properly.

Doctors prescribed three remedies: physical therapy, corrective shoes during the day, and a special brace at night. "I remember the brace," Kristi said, "because it hurt so bad." Fortunately, Kristi's ailment, although severe, did not require surgery.

Kristi didn't think of her physical obstacles as she put on figure skates for the first time. "I remember begging my mom to take me skating when I was about six and I loved it," Kristi says. "I would race around the rink with my mom holding me up most of the time." Kristi loved the feeling of movement and speed over the ice.

"Dorothy Hamill had just won the gold medal and I thought someday that could be me," Kristi recalls. She received a Dorothy Hamill doll as a gift and toted the tiny likeness of the skating star wherever she went. "Once in a while, if I was allowed, I'd take the doll on the ice with me," Kristi said.

"We were shopping and there was an ice rink in the mall," Carole Yamaguchi remembers. "We went to an ice show and Kristi fell in love with it!"

In first grade, Kristi began group lessons and quickly learned the basics of figure skating: spinning, crossovers, and spirals. She learned about jumps, such as the axel and salchow, named for the skaters (Axel Paulsen and Ulrich Salchow) who created them.

Kristi also learned how to fall. To stay balanced, ice skaters bend their knees slightly and hold their shoulders straight. Yet even the best skaters fall. When they do, they try to relax and "go with the fall."

Her parents bought Kristi sturdy leather figure skates with one-eighth-inch metal blades. She learned to avoid serious injury by stretching her muscles. After carefully lacing her new skates, Kristi moved slowly around the rink until she felt warm.

Kristi was always small (she weighed only 5 pounds, 15 ounces at birth), but she was strong and flexible. Her compact body was perfectly suited to jumping. She used the "toe picks" (teethlike notches at the front of each blade) to help her leap into the air.

Kristi first learned the easiest jump—the bunny hop. She skipped from one foot and landed on the other. She advanced to the waltz jump, completing a half revolution in the air. She progressed to the axel jump—she jumped forward from one foot, turned 1½ revolutions, and landed backward on the other foot.

Christy Kjarsgaard was teaching private lessons to young skaters in northern California when Kristi signed up as a student. Kristi immediately liked her teacher. She had a gentle manner and an encouraging smile.

Kristi was an eager student, quiet and dedicated. She loved to learn new skills, and she quickly progressed in her lessons. "I don't think Kristi ever thinks of being tired," Kjarsgaard told Kristi's mother.

With Kjarsgaard's private instruction, Kristi learned to spin faster. She pulled her arms close to her body and tried not to become dizzy. "After a little practice, spinning becomes easy, almost second nature," Kristi said.

Kristi practiced as much as she could, although "patches" of ice (sections of an ice rink reserved for certain skaters) were difficult to find after school. The rinks were crowded in the late afternoon with hockey players, advanced students, and recreational skaters.

In 1978, when she was only seven years old, Kristi competed in her first local competition. Onlookers encouraged the Yamaguchis to hire a tutor and adjust Kristi's school schedule so she could devote more time to skating. Kristi's parents refused. She attended regular school and received no special privileges at home. The Yamaguchis wanted Kristi to be a well-adjusted person, not just a figure skater.

Skaters who want to enter competitions must pass compulsory (or "school figure") tests. These tests show how well skaters control the edges, or sharp corners, of each ice skate blade. Using the edges of her blades, Kristi traced and retraced circles and loops onto the ice during practice. At competitions she would be judged on whether the patterns were deep and the circles uniform.

Kristi joined the Palomares Figure Skating Club, a member of the United States Figure Skating Association (USFSA). The USFSA sponsors and regulates competitions, raises money for skating events, and tests skaters. As skaters advance in skill level, they move through divisions established by the USFSA: juvenile, intermediate, novice, junior, and senior.

In December 1980, Kristi entered her first USFSA event, the Central Pacific Regional Championships. She was judged on both her school figures and the creative "free skating" portion of the competition, which is performed to music. Kristi skated skillfully against other girls in the pre-juvenile division and placed fifth.

At age 11, Kristi had progressed to the USFSA's juvenile division. At the 1982 Central Pacific Championships, she placed fifth in her grouping. She also met Rudi Galindo, a 13-year-old skater from San Jose, California, at the event. He was looking for a pairs partner. Pairs skaters perform side-by-side leaps and spins. The man also lifts the woman overhead and launches her in "throw jumps."

"I was looking for someone as small as me," Rudi said after he met Kristi. "She was perfect." Coach Jim Hulick, a former pairs champion, thought Kristi and Rudi were a good match. He asked the Yamaguchis if he could oversee the team's training. Kristi's parents agreed.

At age 12, Kristi was skating in both singles and pairs competitions. She and Rudi joined the St. Moritz Ice Skating Club. Kristi passed her intermediate test and worked hard at practice.

Rudi hoists Kristi overhead at an early competition.

She and Rudi skated well at regional competitions throughout 1984. By 1985 the team had advanced from the novice to the junior pairs division, and Kristi had become a novice singles skater. Skaters who perform well at the regional level advance to sectional competitions. Top skaters at sectionals (Eastern, Midwestern, and Pacific Coast) qualify for the National Championships.

Kristi was determined to skate at Nationals. At the 1985 Pacific Coast Sectionals, Kristi skated an artistic program that included a triple toe loop/double toe loop combination jump and a high triple salchow.

She waited with her parents as the judges' scores were announced. Kristi's wish came true—she had won the novice title and would skate at the 1985 National Championships in Kansas City, Missouri.

3
Ice Time

Figure skating was no longer just a challenging hobby for Kristi. Despite her parents' earlier restrictions, 14-year-old Kristi modified her class schedule and studied with a tutor so that she had time to practice and travel to competitions.

Skaters who win medals at Nationals represent the United States every year at the World Championships. National medalists compete every four years at the Olympic Games!

Kristi was excited to attend her first National Championships, and she learned a lot there. Watching the more experienced pairs skaters perform, Kristi became nervous. A fall during a pairs routine can injure one or both partners. She saw one man drop his partner from an overhead lift! Luckily, Kristi and Rudi skated well, placing fifth in junior pairs.

Kristi and Rudi perform the sit spin (top) and the camel (bottom).
Pairs skating involves teamwork and precision.

20

Kristi also discovered one frustrating aspect of competitive skating—subjective judging. Judges attend workshops on scoring, yet their rankings, or "ordinals," are often based on personal preference. Kristi narrowly missed winning the bronze medal in the women's novice division. One judge's ordinal cost her the medal. Still, she was pleased with her first experience at Nationals and headed home to rest.

Later that year, Kristi and Rudi received exciting news from the USFSA. They were invited to skate in their first international event—the World Junior Championships in Sarajevo, Yugoslavia. Displaying their skills before judges from many nations, Kristi and Rudi skated well enough to place fifth.

At the 1986 Nationals on Long Island, New York, Kristi and Rudi, in matching red costumes, stunned the audience with their unique "mirror" skating. Their side-by-side triple jumps and camel spins—performed in opposite directions—created a mirrorlike effect. The crowd gave a rousing cheer when the pair finished.

The results were announced: Kristi Yamaguchi and Rudi Galindo were the 1986 junior pairs champions. Kristi couldn't believe it—she and Rudi had been skating together for only three years. They were the highest ranked junior pairs team in the nation. Their partnership was headed for the top!

Kristi was also on her way. In the junior women's

event, Kristi's strong free skating helped her rise from 11th place after the school figures to 4th place overall.

She and Rudi attended three more competitions in 1986: the Olympic Festival (third place), Skate America (fifth place), and Junior Worlds (third place). With their coaches, Kristi and Rudi participated in a special event at the Olympic Training Center in Colorado Springs, Colorado. The skaters were tested for endurance, measured for growth, and taught new training techniques.

At the 1987 Nationals in Tacoma, Washington, Kristi and Rudi competed for the first time in the senior pairs division. They received an enthusiastic reception for their action-packed program and skated to a promising fifth-place finish.

Kristi also won the silver medal in the women's junior division in Tacoma. After Nationals Kristi was chosen to represent the United States at the Merano Spring Trophy, an international competition in Italy. She competed in Europe and came home with a gold medal.

The 1988 Olympics were only six months away. The USFSA invited Kristi and other skaters to compete as teams, not individuals, in the Olympic Festival in North Carolina. Kristi's team won both gold and bronze medals. She had fun as a member of a squad, without the pressure of winning a title.

Kristi and Rudi (far left) have fun with other skaters at the U.S. Olympic Festival.

Kristi's string of successes continued at the 1987 Junior Worlds in Brisbane, Australia. Kristi won the women's title, and she and Rudi won the junior pairs. This was the last time she would compete as a junior skater as her skills now permitted her to skate among the best amateurs—at the senior level.

At the 1988 National Championships in Denver, Colorado, Kristi vied with the finest skaters in the country—including Debi Thomas and Jill Trenary. The three medalists would represent the United States at the 1988 Winter Olympics in Calgary, Alberta, Canada. In a tough field of seasoned contenders, Kristi placed 13th in the school figures, 8th in free skating, and 10th overall.

Coach Kjarsgaard guided Kristi's career from the beginning.

In senior pairs, Kristi and Rudi performed well in the "short program" (a two-minute free-skating routine with required elements). The night of the "long program," or finals, was very exciting. The top three teams would win medals and go to the Olympics.

Kristi prepared as usual. "I save my energy for that night," she explained. "I usually try to take a nap. Just thinking about the competition makes me sleepy!" Kristi and Rudi went to the rink early to warm up and rehearse their routine. They came close to winning a medal that evening—placing fifth. Coach Jim Hulick knew their fortunes would improve since many top teams retire or turn professional after the Olympics.

Kristi's busy year continued. She competed at Skate Electric in England, Skate America, and the NHK Trophy in Japan. Kristi had a realistic chance to earn a spot on the world championship team at the 1989 Nationals in Baltimore, Maryland. Only two American women would be eligible to skate at Worlds in the women's division. Kristi hoped to be one of them.

Before Nationals, ABC-TV taped an "Up Close and Personal" segment to introduce Kristi to its viewers. The cameras recorded her training with Christy Kjarsgaard at 5:00 A.M., practicing lifts with Rudi, and shopping with her friends.

"I skate because I love skating," Kristi says. "Sometimes I ask myself, 'Why do I compete?' But I never say, 'Why do I skate?'"

Kristi was excited to think millions of people would watch her on television. She had to skate well at Nationals or the segment wouldn't be broadcast. Jill Trenary, the 1987 national champion, was the favorite to win the title.

Olympic gold medalists Peggy Fleming (1968) and Brian Boitano (1988) were TV commentators for the event. "Kristi is creative and technically above the other challengers," Boitano said. Kristi is "gorgeous to watch," Fleming added.

Kristi and Rudi tried to block out all the media attention as they skated the pairs short program. They completed strong double axels and performed the "death spiral"—Rudi held Kristi's hand as she leaned backward over the ice, skating on one edge. They received second-place rankings, behind Natalie and Wayne Seybold.

Christy Kjarsgaard worried that Kristi's dual practice and performance schedule would make her tired. Kjarsgaard also worried that Kristi wouldn't perform well in the school figures. Judges often had a difficult time seeing Kristi's faint tracings on the ice. Kjarsgaard was relieved when Kristi held fourth place after the women's school figures and short program.

The long program of the pairs event was held one night before the women's finals. As other singles competitors relaxed, 17-year-old Kristi put on her dark blue competition costume and listened to a tape of her music.

Waiting backstage, Kristi heard the crowd moan when a team fell and applaud loudly when a pair performed well. She knew the great skaters "worked a crowd," encouraging spectators to take part in a performance. Kristi loved an enthusiastic crowd clapping along to her music. She kept this in mind as she and Rudi warmed up near the end of the rink.

Kristi and Rudi's rise to the top of pairs skating was swift.

As the announcer introduced them, Kristi and Rudi glided to their starting positions in the center of the Baltimore Arena—filled with more than 10,000 people. They began their 4½-minute program, to music from *Romeo and Juliet*, by successfully completing side-by-side triple jumps— the flip and the toe loop. The crowd applauded each clean lift and throw jump.

"This program is simply wonderful, absolutely thrilling," announcer Dick Button said. At the end of the routine, the crowd roared its approval. Kristi and Rudi hugged each other. They skated over to Jim Hulick and waited for their scores.

Nine judges each assign two scores after a performance. The first score is for technical merit (difficulty of maneuvers, mastery of jumps and spins). The second score is for artistic impression (musical interpretation, style, and dance arrangement). The highest score—a perfect 6.0—is rare.

Kristi and Rudi received three 5.7's and six 5.8's for technical merit and two 5.7's and seven 5.8's for artistic impression. The Seybolds did not skate well and received lower scores. It was official—Kristi Yamaguchi and Rudi Galindo were the 1989 national pairs champions. They were on their way to Worlds in Paris, France!

Less than 24 hours later, skating to Offenbach's "Gâité Parisienne," Kristi completed seven difficult triple jumps. Petite Kristi, only 4 feet, 11 inches tall, was fearless as she attacked her jumps. Of all the women, she skated the most challenging program.

The crowd gave her a standing ovation, and the judges awarded her scores of 5.7 to 5.9. Kristi won the long program. She had skipped from eighth in school figures and fourth after the short program to second overall. She had almost beaten Jill Trenary!

Kristi received the silver medal, a spot on the world championship team, and a place in history. She became the first woman to win a medal in two events at Nationals since Margaret Graham in 1954.

Kristi was overjoyed for herself and for Rudi, but most of all for their coach, Jim Hulick. While Kristi and Rudi were training to become champions, their coach was fighting his own battles. In August 1988, doctors discovered Jim had cancer. They began chemotherapy treatments—hoping to destroy the cancer with powerful chemicals.

In December 1988, doctors found a tumor growing in Jim's chest. Jim knew his disease might prevent him from seeing Kristi and Rudi win the titles they had worked so hard to achieve.

Jim hadn't told his prize pupils about his illness. He didn't want to worry them. After Nationals Jim finally explained his situation to Kristi and Rudi.

The "death spiral" is thrilling to watch but scary to perform.

He was proud of them and wanted to go to the World Championships. When his doctors gave him permission to travel, Jim was elated and said, "I feel like all my prayers were answered. I'm in ecstasy."

4
Fancy Footwork

Kristi's trip to the 1989 World Championships in Paris, France, was big news. She was profiled in *Sports Illustrated* and *People* magazines. Reporters described Kristi as "a skating sprite with a towering talent."

Kristi felt relaxed as she watched skaters from many countries practice. She saw beautiful Soviet pairs skaters, graceful French ice dancers, and the athletic Japanese. She juggled practice sessions and competed in both singles and pairs events.

Kristi placed sixth overall in the women's division but ranked fourth in free skating. She and Rudi placed fifth in pairs. Although she didn't win a medal, Kristi was invited to skate in the Exhibition of Champions. "Kristi's dazzling smile captivated the international audience...which fell under the spell of this young American," said one CBS-TV commentator.

Kristi relaxes at home with her parents.

Back home Kristi's typical day began at 4:00 A.M. She was on the ice by 5:00 and trained until 10:00—first alone and then with Rudi. She had returned to regular classes at Mission San Jose High School. "I started to feel isolated and thought it would be good to be with kids my age," Kristi said. After attending school, Kristi came home to eat dinner, do homework, and watch TV before bed at 7:30 P.M.

"Kristi is superhuman," Jim Hulick said. "She has endless strength and natural talent—something no one can teach."

"The busier Kristi is the better she does," Carole Yamaguchi added.

Before graduation in June 1989, Kristi's classmates gave her a varsity letter jacket to honor her athletic achievements. "I was lucky to attend normal high school for two years," Kristi said. "I didn't take part in extracurricular activities because I didn't have time. I didn't mind because skating was more important to me."

Graduation was just one of many exciting events for Kristi in 1989. The Women's Sports Foundation named her the "Up and Coming Athlete in Artistic Sports," and readers of *Skating* magazine voted Kristi "Amateur Skater of the Year." After her 18th birthday in July, Kristi was a bridesmaid at Christy Kjarsgaard's wedding to Andrew Ness, a doctor who practices sports medicine.

The marriage meant that Kjarsgaard-Ness would be moving to Edmonton, Alberta, Canada, where Dr. Ness worked. The day after graduation, Kristi moved away from home for the first time. She would train at the Royal Glenora Club in Edmonton and live in Christy and Andrew's home.

"Everyone is really nice and made me feel welcome," Kristi said after moving to Edmonton.

Canadian Kurt Browning, the world champion, also trained at Royal Glenora. He welcomed Kristi and introduced her to the other skaters. Rudi Galindo and Jim Hulick traveled to Edmonton, when their schedules allowed, to work with Kristi on pairs routines.

Despite her happy adjustment in Canada, Kristi's schedule was often stressful. "It's hard when I go home and have to leave the next day for a competition," she explained. "Sometimes I think, God …can't I just stay for a week and get familiar with my room again?"

There were more transitions in 1989, including a major change in the scoring of figure skating. New rules, established by the International Skating Union (ISU), would eliminate school figures from competitions entirely by July 1990. Until then the value of school figures would be reduced from 30 percent of a skater's total score to 20 percent.

Finally, Kristi confronted another change—the horrible realization that Jim Hulick might not live much longer. Jim had become thinner and weaker, yet he insisted on coaching his pairs team. He knew they had an excellent chance at the next World Championships.

"This whole year has been hard for the pair because Jim goes to Los Angeles for his cancer treatments," Kristi said. "We've had to push, for ourselves, but also for him. . . . His treatment has to be put ahead of our skating. He always told us, 'You two keep at it, you could become real superstars someday!'"

The pair practiced new routines, choreographed to musical selections from *3001 Salsoul*, *Magic Bird of Fire*, and *Escape to Coppelia*. New costumes, ivory-colored and beaded, gave Jim's skaters a more mature look.

Coach Jim Hulick demanded the best from his pairs team.

After performances at the Olympic Festival, Skate America, and Skate Canada, Jim accompanied Kristi and Rudi to Kobe, Japan, for the NHK Trophy. Unfortunately, the young pair narrowly missed a medal, placing fourth. Kristi, however, won the silver medal in the women's competition.

Two weeks after Kristi and Rudi returned home, on December 10, 1989, 38-year-old Jim Hulick died. He had fought his battle with cancer for 16 months. "Jim seemed to push his illness aside and focus more on us," Kristi said. "He came to Canada with Rudi to work with us. . . . I think he sacrificed a lot of his health for our skating.

"Our entire pair career is dedicated to Jim," she continued. "He started us out and was with us the last seven years of his life. . . . He made us into what we are right now."

Jim's good friend, Coach John Nicks of California, offered to train Kristi and Rudi so they could defend their title at the 1990 Nationals. Tai Babilonia, a former world pairs champion, gave Kristi a special heart-shaped earring. "It symbolizes hope and strength and I never take it off," Kristi said. Tai understood the pressures Kristi would face at Nationals and hoped the gift would bring her luck.

Kristi wondered if all the changes during the

past year would affect her performance. At the 1990 Nationals in Salt Lake City, Utah, Kristi traced her school figures for the judges. When they finished looking at her etchings, she was only in fifth place.

Kristi was determined to rally back in the short program (now renamed the original program)—she wanted to go to the World Championships. Kristi completed a difficult combination—a triple lutz/double toe loop—which helped her win the original program. The battle for first place was once again between Kristi and Jill Trenary.

Kristi and Rudi competed in the pairs competition before the women's final. "They've matured tremendously this year with a lot more speed, control, and confidence," Peggy Fleming remarked. Kristi's only fall occurred as she tried to land a triple flip. Marks of 5.8 and 5.9, however, assured Kristi and Rudi a second national championship.

The next day, Kristi fell at practice and seemed to lack energy. She skated her long program, to *Swan Lake*, in a pale pink costume. She changed a triple combination jump into a safer double, fell on a triple salchow, and put her hand on the ice to prevent a fall during the loop. "An unusually poor performance," said Dick Button.

Despite her falls, Kristi's marks of 5.5 to 5.8 were high enough to give her the silver medal.

"I'm a little bit disappointed," she said afterward. "I could have been stronger but hopefully there is next year."

Reporters wondered if Kristi's schedule was too demanding. Most skaters specialize in one event. Kristi had to master twice as many routines as her opponents. "Training for both pairs and singles is tough. But I've been doing it for so long.... I think I can do it," Kristi said.

Kristi was disappointed at the 1990 World Figure Skating Championships in Halifax, Nova Scotia, Canada. Jill Trenary won the women's title; Japan's Midori Ito, the silver medalist, was declared the best free skater; and Kristi's teammate Holly Cook was a surprise bronze medalist. Kristi finished in fourth place.

Despite good showings in the original and long programs, Kristi's ninth-place finish in school figures prevented her from winning a medal. She knew the ISU's decision to eliminate school figures would help her in future events.

Kristi and Rudi received another fifth-place ranking in the pairs competition. The Olympics were only two years away. Kristi realized her singles career might be hurt by additional training in pairs. After an exhibition tour, Kristi and Rudi announced their retirement as a team.

"I will miss pairs," Kristi said. "It's a whole

chapter of my life ending....There was no way I could skate at the level I wanted to...competing in both.

"We accomplished as much as we could together," she added. "To improve in one or the other, I had to choose." Rudi resumed competing as a singles skater, and Kristi went back to train in Canada.

As of 1990, Kristi would skate solo.

Kristi performs a beautiful spiral.

5
To the Top

Kristi soon realized that her decision to compete only in singles was the correct choice. At the 1990 Goodwill Games in Tacoma, Washington, she took first place over world champion Jill Trenary. She also defeated Midori Ito at the Skate America competition in Buffalo, New York. Kristi's long program, to music from *Samson and Delilah*, included seven triple jumps. She received a standing ovation and marks of 5.7 to 5.9.

Kristi's winning streak continued at the Nations Cup competition in Gelsenkirchen, Germany. "Once she made up her mind to concentrate on singles," Christy Kjarsgaard-Ness explained, "everything came into focus."

Before the 1991 Nationals in Minneapolis, Minnesota, Kristi found time to skate at two fun events. In October 1990, she traveled to Alexandria, Virginia, to help Dorothy Hamill kick off

National Ice-Skating Month. On January 1, 1991, she skated at the Tournament of Roses parade in Pasadena, California.

Kristi's chances of winning Nationals in February were better than ever. School figures had been eliminated, and Jill Trenary had withdrawn due to an injury. Kristi easily won the original program and became the favorite to win the overall title.

Although she fell on a triple salchow, *Sports Illustrated* called Kristi's long program "mesmerizing." Kristi received marks of 5.7 to 5.9 from the judges and then watched the next skater, Tonya Harding.

Tonya, only 45 seconds into her program, completed the historic triple axel. The 3½-revolution jump had never been performed by an American woman in competition! Japan's Midori Ito was the first woman to land the jump—at the 1989 Worlds.

Tonya went on to complete six other triple jumps, and the crowd gave her a standing ovation. The judges awarded her higher marks than Kristi's—and the national championship.

Kristi and her coach were devastated. This was the third year in a row she had narrowly missed the gold. "Nationals are just one competition," she said. "I have to keep my spirits up and think of the World Championships as a new experience."

After Nationals Kristi trained harder than ever in

Canada. Kurt Browning helped Kristi rehearse her programs until both skaters were exhausted. "We would drive together and Kurt said to me, 'You deserve to win.' He would ask, 'Do you realize, there could be two world champions in this car?'" Kristi recalls.

At the 1991 World Championships in Munich, Germany, Kristi was thrilled to watch Kurt win his third gold medal. She then concentrated on her own performance, skating a near-perfect original program. She was in first place heading into the long program. The title was Kristi's to win or lose.

In a red chiffon outfit, and skating last among the women, Kristi landed all seven triple jumps except one—the triple salchow. Skillfully gliding through the rest of her program, Kristi knew she had skated well.

When the scores were announced, Kristi screamed in delight. Her technical marks included five 5.9's. Her artistic marks included seven 5.9's and her first 6.0! She won the gold medal. Christy Kjarsgaard-Ness hugged the new world champion. All their years of work together had resulted in this night.

"It's still hard to believe," Kristi said. "I'm the world champion!" Kristi and her teammates—silver medalist Tonya Harding and bronze medalist Nancy Kerrigan—had swept the medals for the United States.

Tonya Harding, Kristi, and Nancy Kerrigan finished on top at Worlds. Never before had three women swept the medals for one nation.

The 1992 Winter Olympics were 11 months away. So much had to be done for the upcoming season. With the help of her coach, Kristi picked music for her new programs. She selected Johann Strauss's "Blue Danube Waltz" for the original program and Ernesto Lecuona's crowd-pleasing "Malaguena" for the long program.

In Edmonton Dr. Ness developed a weight-training program to help strengthen the muscles in Kristi's legs. In July 1990, Kristi traveled to Toronto, Ontario, Canada, to work with chore-ographer Sandra Bezic on inventive new routines.

Finally, Kristi traveled to costume designer Lauren Sheehan's house in Enid, Oklahoma. "I think it's important to create the entire mood of the program," Kristi said. "People come to watch figure skating because it's a beautiful sport and the costumes are just part of it."

Kristi seemed distracted during the pre-Olympic season. She placed second—to Tonya Harding at Skate America in Oakland, California, and to Midori Ito at the Trophee Lalique in Albertville, France. Kristi knew only the three medalists at Nationals in Orlando, Florida, would represent the United States at the 1992 Olympics.

Arriving in Orlando with her mom, Kristi was the center of the media's attention. When reporters asked Kristi about her years of training and dedication, she was quick to thank her mom and dad. "My parents have worked hard and made a lot of sacrifices," she said.

"There have been financial sacrifices to get where we are," Kristi's mother added. "We all drive old cars with over 160,000 miles."

Kristi's final program at Nationals appeared effortless and controlled. She wasn't even bothered when the bow in her hair fell onto the ice during the triple toe loop. She performed all seven of her triple jumps, including the triple salchow.

Kristi often had trouble completing the triple salchow, so her mom promised her $100 if she could land the jump. "Going into the jump, I thought, 'Just do it and get the hundred bucks,'"

Kristi recalls. "No matter what, I was going to land that jump!"

The crowd stood as Kristi finished her performance. "This is the best I've ever skated at Nationals," she said, waiting for her scores. "I know I probably have a place on the [Olympic] team," she added modestly.

The results were announced: Kristi won the gold medal, Nancy Kerrigan captured the silver, and Tonya Harding earned the bronze. Each skater won a berth on the Olympic team, and Kristi was finally named national champion. Her scores included a perfect 6.0!

"All the early mornings do start to pay off," Kristi said before the Olympics. "You stay in it, stay focused, and in the end things work out."

6
Champion

Immediately before the 1992 Winter Olympics, the media focused on Kristi Yamaguchi. *TV Guide* and *Newsweek* magazines placed Kristi's photograph on their covers. One headline described her as a "Jewel on Ice."

Kristi's main rival for the gold medal was expected to be Midori Ito of Japan. Midori, an athletic skater and powerful jumper, could land the triple axel (a move Kristi couldn't master). "Kristi is graceful and musical," Dorothy Hamill said, "but when Midori skates, she has me on the edge of my seat."

"It would be nice to have the triple axel because other girls have it," Kristi said. "I've been working on my other jumps, connected with different moves, and the overall program...rather than just doing the tricks."

The competition between Midori and Kristi was billed as "the athlete versus the artist." Andrew Ness said, "It's going to be a real fight."

The 16th Winter Olympic Games began with the lighting of the Olympic torch on February 8, 1992, in Albertville, France. More than 2,000 athletes from 65 countries were entered in events held throughout the French Alps.

"The Olympics are a dream," Kristi said, "everything I expected.... It's a thrill walking out with the entire American team and being in the Olympic Village." She and roommate Nancy Kerrigan had to wait 11 days before their competition began. They cheered teammate Paul Wylie as he won the silver medal in the men's competition.

Lack of available ice time in Albertville permitted Kristi only 1½ hours a day to practice. Her coach made plans for Kristi to travel to Megeve, France, so she could train more. "The training has been good," Kristi said. "I hope next week goes as smoothly."

"This Olympics will be unique," Kristi said. "It's so unpredictable. No one woman has dominated the field the past four years—we've had three different world champions and three different national champions. Whoever puts on the performance of the year will win it."

Midori Ito was favored in Albertville.

Kristi's original program was choreographed to "The Blue Danube," a waltz she loves. "It's strong music," she remarked, "so I have to move strongly to it." On February 19, Kristi dressed in a sequined, blue-chiffon costume. To an emotional cheer from the crowd, she began her two-minute program.

Kristi performed each of the eight required elements to near perfection. The first, a triple lutz/double toe loop, was beautiful! She followed this with a double flip jump (with one hand held above her head) and a layback spin (holding her skate with one hand). She glided gracefully into a spiral, a circular step sequence, and a combination camel/layback/sit spin. Kristi landed a high, clean double axel and finished with a final spin. The audience cheered and threw flowers onto the ice!

As the marks were posted, Christy Kjarsgaard-Ness hugged her student. Kristi pretended to wipe perspiration off her forehead. Whew. What a relief! The judges awarded her seven 5.8's, one 5.7, and one 5.6 for artistic impression. She received seven 5.9's and two 5.8's for technical merit. She was in first place.

Kristi watched the other skaters on a monitor backstage. Nancy Kerrigan skated well and ranked second. French skater Surya Bonaly gave a lively performance and ranked third. Midori Ito fell on a combination jump. Kristi was shocked. Midori was in fourth place heading into the finals.

The next day, Kristi practiced her final program. She felt focused, completed all her jumps, and then went to an outdoor cafe for lunch with her parents. "It's been fun having my family here," Kristi said as she prepared a crepe for her dad. "I'm glad we're able to share the Olympics together." The night before the finals, Kristi left the athletes' village and stayed with her parents and her sister, Lori, in Albertville. Brother Brett had to stay home in California for basketball games and school.

The morning of February 21, Kristi rehearsed her long program in a red, white, and blue outfit. A curious crowd paid just to see her practice. After a light lunch with her family and a nap, Kristi dressed in a long-sleeved, gold-and-black costume. She tied a gold ribbon in her hair.

Then Kristi went with her mom to the Hall of Ice. Dorothy Hamill and Brian Boitano came to see her backstage. Dorothy kissed and hugged Kristi, wishing her the best of luck. More than 9,000 spectators, including Kristi's dad and sister, waited in the stands.

The warm-up began and Kristi tried to get comfortable on the ice. She had to warm up quickly because she was first, among the top skaters, to perform. The TV lights were bright on the ice. Photographers and reporters looked on as the crowd cheered Kristi and the other skaters practicing their jumps.

Kristi's name was announced. She heard the applause as she skated to the center of the ice. Taking her position, she listened for the music. Kristi remembered what Christy Kjarsgaard-Ness had taught her. She thought of Lori, Brett, her mom and dad, and the years spent training for this moment.

Kristi's 4-minute, 10-second program began with the audience clapping along to the music. They cheered as she completed her difficult triple combination jumps. Kristi landed a triple flip and glided into an elegant spiral. She seemed relaxed as she leaped into the triple loop. Then, to her surprise, Kristi fell out of the jump. Shaken, she changed the next jump, a triple salchow, into a double. She didn't want to make another mistake.

Three and a half minutes into her program, Kristi landed a triple lutz and her last jump, a double axel. Spinning to a conclusion, Kristi smiled and waved. The crowd gave her a thunderous ovation.

Kristi worried that the judges would penalize her for the one mistake. Yet the scores, five 5.7's and four 5.8's in technical merit and one 5.8 and eight 5.9's for artistic impression, were strong.

"I became a little cautious in the slow portion," Kristi said about her fall. "I didn't go into it as positive as I should have and it showed."

After Nancy Kerrigan skated, Kristi was still in first place. She and her coach held hands while watching Midori Ito perform. Midori fell on her famous triple axel but completed the jump on a second attempt. When Midori's scores appeared, Kristi still held the lead. She had won the Olympic gold medal!

Tearfully happy, she hugged Christy and Andrew Ness. Cameras flashed. Everyone wanted to congratulate the new Olympic champion.

"I didn't think of medals once I was skating," Kristi said. "I wanted to take one thing at a time. . . . So many things went through my mind:

Golden girl!

Can this be happening right now? Is it my time? I still can't believe it!"

The medal ceremonies began. The announcer said, "Olympic champion Kristi Yamaguchi." Kristi skated to the center of the ice. She bowed to the crowd and beamed at her parents and sister. The president of the International Olympic Committee gave Kristi the sparkling crystal-and-gold medal.

Kristi shook hands with silver medalist Midori Ito and hugged bronze medalist Nancy Kerrigan. The American flag was raised as the national anthem was played. "Everything has been so overwhelming since I stepped off the ice," Kristi said later. "Standing there while they played the national anthem was incredible. It's all just been a whirlwind."

The next day, after watching a hockey game, Kristi and the other champions skated an exhibition. "The United States has waited 16 years for an Olympic gold medalist in the ladies' event," said veteran skater Scott Hamilton, "and we've got a great one."

The Games were over, and the athletes took a bus to the closing ceremonies. Kristi brought along a video recorder to tape the event. "I'll never forget the Olympics," she said. "It's the best experience of my life."

After the Olympics, Kristi received extraordinary attention in the United States. Her photograph appeared on the cover of *Sports Illustrated*. Fan mail (500 letters a week) arrived at her house. "It was a little weird to be home after the Olympics," she said. "So many people recognize me now...it's hard to believe."

Kristi found many financial opportunities after the Games. Described as a "hot commodity" by

Newsday newspaper, she hired a management firm to handle her business ventures. Kristi signed contracts to endorse Evian bottled water, Ray-Ban sunglasses, DuraSoft contact lenses, and Kraft-Philadelphia cream cheese. She modeled fashions in *Vogue* and *Seventeen* magazines for Hoechst Celanese, a fabric company. Her picture appeared on Kellogg's cereal boxes.

Next, Kristi participated in the Tour of Champions with Paul Wylie, Nancy Kerrigan, and other Olympic skaters. They performed in 42 cities in the United States. The tour gave Kristi an opportunity to polish her exhibition skills, relax with her fellow competitors, and visit places she had never seen. She saw Broadway plays in New York City, visited Elvis Presley's home in Memphis, and danced at Hollywood's Spago nightclub.

Kristi's world began to change. She turned professional and joined the "Stars on Ice" show—receiving the largest salary in tour history. She also won more than $80,000 in prize money at two competitions and bought a home in Reno, Nevada.

Kristi was named the official spokesperson for the American Lung Association. "I was pretty close with my grandfather, who died of lung cancer," she remarked. "He was a big influence and he made me work harder. It was tough to see him go through the suffering towards the end." Kristi urges young people: "Take care of your health and don't smoke."

At the 1992 Summer Olympics in Barcelona, Spain, Kristi served as a special presidential delegate with Arnold Schwarzenegger and flew on the president's airplane, *Air Force One*. She met athletes Evander Holyfield, Magic Johnson, and Mary Lou Retton. She went dancing with film director Spike Lee.

Kristi visits with talk-show hosts Regis Philbin and Kathie Lee Gifford.

Kristi's success surprised some members of the media. One business magazine thought Kristi's Japanese heritage might lessen her popularity with advertisers. "I was really surprised to hear about the endorsement controversy," Kristi said. "I'm a fourth-generation American. I was born and raised in California...my values are American and I went to the Olympics for the United States."

"Kristi doesn't even speak Japanese," Midori Ito said, "except to say 'good morning.' She's 100 percent American."

Kristi's family history became public knowledge after her selection to the Olympic team. During World War II, after Japan bombed Pearl Harbor in Hawaii, many residents became afraid and suspicious of Americans of Japanese origin. This fear grew into such hostility that the U.S. government took 120,000 Japanese Americans (including Kristi's grandparents) from their homes and put them into prison camps in the western United States. They endured considerable hardship.

Kristi's mother, the former Carole Doi, was born at a camp. Years later, Carole met and married Jim Yamaguchi, who had also spent time in the camps as a child.

Kristi was aware of this situation, yet she also knew that her family did not hold any resentment toward the government. "My grandfather didn't talk much about the war," Kristi explained. "He let me know how proud he was to see me make it as an Asian American representing the United States."

"We are proud Americans," Jim Yamaguchi added. "I think when somebody of our background is up there on that stand, singing the national anthem, it says something about America."

"I feel very lucky about how everything has gone so far in my life," Kristi says today. Her advice for other young people is simple. "If you have a dream like I had, it's really important to put the work into it. Some days you wake up and think 'I just can't do this,' but you look beyond the training and it pushes you. Dedicate yourself to achieving those goals. Then...no matter what happens, the feeling of reaching your personal best is fulfilling."

FIGURE SKATING TERMS AND MOVES

axel: a jump in which the skater takes off going forward, turns 1½ times, and lands backward on the other foot

bunny hop: a jump in which the skater takes off going forward and lands forward on the other foot

camel: a spin in the spiral position, with the free leg held parallel to the ice and the arms outstretched

combination jump: two jumps performed one after another, without footwork performed in between

crossover: a move performed while skating forward or backward, in which the skater lifts one foot off the ice and places it over the skating leg

death spiral: a pairs move in which the man holds the woman's outstretched arm and pivots in place. She spirals around him on one skate, while leaning backward and parallel to the ice.

edges: the bottom corners of the ice skate blade. Skaters use their edges to carve figures in the ice.

flip: a jump in which the skater takes off going backward—using the toe pick of the free skate to push off from the ice—turns one time, and lands backward on the other foot

free skating: the creative portion of a skating competition, performed to music and including jumps, spins, and footwork

layback: a spin performed with the back arched and arms outstretched

long program: the final performance of the free skating event, lasting approximately four minutes and involving the skater's choice of jumps, spins, and dance moves

loop: a jump in which the skater takes off going backward, turns one time, and lands backward on the same foot

lutz: a jump—similar to the flip—in which the skater takes off going backward—using the toe pick of the free skate to push off from the ice—turns one time, and lands backward on the other foot

salchow: a jump in which the skater takes off going backward, turns one time, and lands backward on the other foot

school figures: set patterns based on the figure eight that skaters must carve for judges to view. Eliminated after the 1991 season from singles competition, school figures are now a separate event.

short program: the first performance of the free skating event, lasting approximately two minutes and including required skating elements

sit spin: a spin performed in the squat position, on one skate with the free leg extended in front of the body

spiral: a move in which the skater glides on one foot with the free leg extended

throw jumps: jumps performed in pairs skating, in which the male partner lifts and launches the female partner into her jump

toe loop: a jump in which the skater takes off going backward—using the toe pick of the free skate to push off from the ice—turns one time, and lands backward on the same foot

waltz: a jump in which the skater takes off going forward, makes a half turn, and lands backward on the other foot

ACKNOWLEDGMENTS

Photographs used with permission of Shiobhan Donohue except p. 9, Photofest; pp. 12, 34, *The Argus* (courtesy of the Yamaguchi family); pp. 17, 37, Paul Harvath; pp. 46, 55, Tom Treick/*The Oregonian;* p. 51, Lois Elfman.